Painting Canvas
For Hobby

A Beginner's Painting Guide With Easy
Painting Lessons On How To Paint On
Canvas So You Can Learn To Create Your
Own Dramatic Canvas Artwork Just Like The
Great Masters!

By:

Sheryll R. Hill

Many artists today use canvas as their painting surface of choice. Good-quality canvas can hold colors very well which helps bring about professional results. Canvas also has very good shelf-life so it can protect the quality of paintings throughout time.

Canvas painting is a popular method but it can be difficult especially for beginner painters. Does this mean then that newbies need to have formal painting lessons to learn the skill? It can help, of course, but painting on canvas can be easy if you have the right guide to teach you proper techniques and helpful tips to use the painting tools and materials.

There are many important lessons for learning canvas painting. First of all, you have to know how to select your medium. You also need to decide what style of painting you will practice on. Then, there is the matter of choosing your colors, how to find your light source and what details to pay attention to so you can paint that on your canvas precisely to capture real life.

This book is a painting lesson written for beginner artists in particular who are interested to learn how to paint on canvas. It is an easy guide which will give you all the most important elements of canvas painting so you can learn on your own and produce impressive canvas works of art for your own pleasure, or possibly sell them for huge profits!

Disclaimer And Terms Of Use Agreement

The author and publisher have used their best efforts in preparing this book. The author and publisher make no representation or warranties with respect to the accuracy, applicability, fitness, or completeness of the contents of this book. The information contained in this book is strictly for educational purposes. Therefore, if you wish to apply ideas contained in this book, you are taking full responsibility for your actions.

Every effort has been made to accurately represent this product and its potential. However, there is no guarantee that you will improve in any way using the techniques and ideas in these materials. Examples in these materials are not to be interpreted as a promise or guarantee of anything. Self-help and improvement potential is entirely dependent on the person using our product, ideas and techniques.

Your level of improvement in attaining the results claimed in our materials depends on the time you devote to the program, ideas and techniques mentioned and knowledge and various skills. Since these factors differ according to individuals, we cannot guarantee your success or improvement level. Nor are we responsible for any of your actions.

Many factors will be important in determining your actual results and no guarantees are made that you will achieve results similar to ours or anybody else's, in fact no guarantees are made that you will achieve any results from our ideas and techniques in our material.

The author and publisher disclaim any warranties (express or implied), merchantability, or fitness for any particular purpose. The author and publisher shall in no event be held liable to any party for any direct, indirect, punitive, special, incidental or other consequential damages arising directly or indirectly from any use of this material, which is provided "as is", and without warranties.

The author and publisher do not warrant the performance, effectiveness or applicability of any sites listed or linked to in this book. All links are for information purposes only and are not warranted for content, accuracy or any other implied or explicit purpose.

Table of Contents

Disclaimer And Terms Of Use Agreement 2

Table of Contents 4

Chapter 1 – Painting Basics 5

Chapter 2 – An Intro To Paints 15

Chapter 3 – Paint Brushes Essentials 18

Chapter 4 – Creating Colors 21

Chapter 5 – Where Is Your Light Source? 24

Chapter 6 – Your Painting Style....................... 27

Chapter 7 – What To Paint About 30

Chapter 8 – A Place To Paint............................ 33

Chapter 9 – Painting Supply Resources........... 36

Chapter 10 – Cleaning Up................................. 39

Chapter 11 – Free Painting Lessons................. 42

Chapter 12 – Caring For Your Artworks 44

Chapter 13 – Attention to Detail 46

Chapter 14 – Your Subject Matters 49

Chapter 15 – Frequently Asked Questions....... 53

Chapter 16 – Art Schools & Programs 58

Chapter 17 – Museums of Fine Art.................. 60

Chapter 18 – The Joy Of Painting 61

Chapter 1 – Painting Basics

People have been expressing themselves through painting for thousands of years. Even the cavemen showed great hunts or other events with paints made from berries and plants. There just seems to be an innate need to show others our thoughts, feelings, and ideas through pictures. The phrase "A picture is worth a thousand words" is so very true.

With colors and design you can express every emotion you feel. Whether it is a woman in a garden waiting for her lover or an old barn set in a field of wild flowers, the subject bring memories and feelings to the fore front of the viewer's mind. All of this being accomplished on a blank canvas with paint.

There are some basics the beginning artist should know. Although you may have been sketching and drawing for years, the first time you pick up a brush it will seem foreign to you. This is fine. You will become very familiar with each of the brushes and the strokes they can make. They will soon be as comfortable in your hand as the charcoal pencil you use on the sketch pad.

Paints can add style and creativity to an art piece. A single tear drop on the face can take on a totally new dimension by adding color. Paints allow you to do this with ease. The types of paint you use will also allow you to be more creative.

Many artists use the oil paints for extend projects. The oils do not dry as quickly and can be rejuvenated with a little turpentine or mineral spirits. This allows the artist to continue the project another day. The brushes you use with an oil painting must be cleaned extremely well. If you allow them to sit in the cleaning solution they can lose their shape. This means you may not be able to use certain brushes to achieve a particular brush stroke.

When the artist uses acrylic paints, the dry time is extremely fast. Many times, a project which is being done in half an hour or so will be done with acrylic paints because of the ease of use. Clean up with soap and water is a quick task. The brushes wash up quickly and cleanly. Allowing them to dry either on a flat surface or standing with bristles up will keep their original shape.

The best thing to do when first beginning canvas painting is to experiment. Try using oils. Become familiar with acrylics. You will eventually choose which medium you prefer to work with. By playing with each, you can determine how the paints mix, get a feel for how they flow onto the canvas, and become familiar with blending. These are all important for the novice artist to consider.

Another factor is the type of canvas you will want to use. There are stretch canvases, rolled canvas, canvas boards, and canvas mats. Each one can be used for different styles, artwork, and even paints. Which one you use will be determined by which one you feel more comfortable painting upon.

The information can become overwhelming when you start painting on canvas. Getting to know the terminology will help clear some things up a little bit. Here are some terms we will be using in this book.

Abstract – abstract art depicts the subject by using form and color. You may see a resemblance to the original piece. However, the subject is generally represented in more geometric shapes than the natural setting.

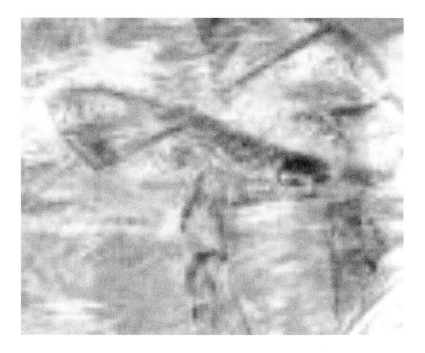

Above are two forms of abstract art.

Accent – Giving exceptional detail to a certain object in the painting to bring attention to it.

A good example of accenting.

Acrylic – A type of paint which dries quickly. It can easily be cleaned up with mineral spirits.

Alla Prima – Meaning "at the first" in Italian, this phrase means the painting is completed with just one sitting.

Cool colors – Colors associated with the cold such as blue.

Color Wheel – Any full spectrum circular diagram which represents the relationships of colors.

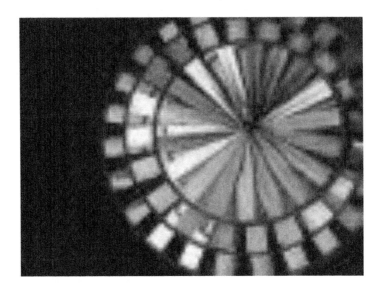

This allows the colors to be compared for contrast.

Composition – The arrangement of the elements in an art piece.

Medium – The type of pain being used to create a work of art. It can also mean the binder, usually oil.

Palette – The painter's board where colors can be mixed and different hues can be created.

 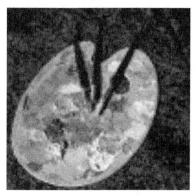

A before and after shot.

Perspective – Being able to reproduce the same height, depth, and distance perception in a two dimensional medium that the human eye would perceive.

This photograph is a good representation of perspective.

Pigment – The colored substance created by natural elements and synthetic ones which are mixed with certain binders to create paints.

Primary colors – A color which cannot be created by mixing other colors. The only three primary colors are red, blue, and yellow. With these three all other colors can be created. (White is not a color. It is the absence of color. Black is the combination of all colors.)

Secondary colors – Any color which can be created from mixing the primary colors, such as violet, green, and orange.

Warm colors – Hues which represent warmth such as orange, red, yellow.

Now that you know some of the language, let's step into the art studio.

Chapter 2 – An Intro To Paints

There are two types of paints which work well on canvas. One is oil and the other is acrylic. You need to choose which painting medium you will be using. Some people prefer the oils to the acrylics. There are several differences between the two paints. The oil can take days to dry completely. This allows the artist to continue with the painting for days after the original sitting. The acrylics are not so forgiving. These paints can dry within hours. If you think you can make a mistake and go back later to fix it, you are wrong.

Oil paints are made up of pigment and oils. A simple paint can be made from dried saffron and peanut oil. Mixed properly you can use this formula to create a wonderful shade of yellow which you could also eat. Most of the oil paints on the market are poisonous, so always keep them out of the hands of children.

When oil paints are made from three things. This is pigment, oil, and some type of drying agent. The latter was added because the oils took too long to dry. Drying agents can be things like paint thinner.

Although the primary colors can be formulated into any other color in the spectrum, there is no need to try creating the same color every time you paint. Oil paints come in any shade or hue you can think of, from black to white. Each color can be blended with another to add even more combinations. There is literally no color you cannot reproduce on the canvas with oil paints.

Oil paints can be used to create textures. They can be spread on thick or thin. One thing you will learn is the more thick you have the paint the longer it will take to dry. Also, a thick layer of oil paint will crack as it dries. This is not good for the painting. The best thing to do when working with oils is to create the work in layers. This will allow the paint to dry evenly and prevent cracking. This is one reason why some artists spend days creating an art piece instead of rushing through alla prima.

Acrylics are synthetic paints designed to mix and blend just like the oils. The main difference is the dry time. While oils can take days, acrylics can take only hours. There are advantages to using acrylics over oils. When you need the project done quickly, the acrylics are up to the task. By having a faster dry time, the painting can have layers added in hours instead of days.

With acrylics, the artist can be assured of a straight line for horizons or other needs. You can actually apply masking tape to dried acrylic paint. When you peel the tape off, there is no danger of lifting the paint off the canvas. This ensures clean, precise lines every time. With oils, you would have to use an edge and still take the chance of smearing the paints.

Some artists prefer acrylics. Some prefer oils. There are those who go back and forth between the two, depending on the project. It is advisable to learn about each one. You should experiment with at least the primary colors to see which you prefer. Everyone should learn all there is to art. By experimenting with the different mediums, you can learn quite a bit.

Chapter 3 – Paint Brushes Essentials

You cannot do very much painting without a brush. Although some people would argue with that statement, for now we will assume you will be using a standard artist's brush. There are as many brushes on the market as there are paints. Some are made better than others. Do not fall under the misconception that more expensive is better. This is not always the case. I have spent $20 on a brush to have the bristles fall out during my first session. I have one brush I have used for four years now that I paid $3.00 for. It is actually the best brush I own, in my opinion.

The first thing you need to know is there are many different types of brushes. Each one is made from different materials for the bristles. You can order sable brushes or hog bristle. There are squirrel brushes. You can buy the synthetic bristle brushes also.

The truth is that most artists will find a particular set of brushes they like and use them consistently. There may be a few times when they alternate. In the long run, most will go back to the one which feels most comfortable in their hand.

You will get a feel for your favorite type of brush the more you paint. There are certain brushes which will give you a particular flow to the paint. You will either like this or you won't. Until you practice with them, you will never know.

The style of the brush can make all the difference when it comes to painting. A fan brush is the perfect instrument to add leaves to distant trees. A liner brush will allow you to paint in the perfect tree limbs on dead trees or winter trees.

It can become overwhelming when trying to determine which brushes to buy. There are brush sets which give you a good selection to start with and are also inexpensive. You may just want to start with two or three good brushes until you further your experience with painting on canvas.

You will definitely want to buy a fan brush, a liner brush, and a flat brush. You will also want to have an angle brush. Each one of these brushes can give you a certain stroke which makes it easier to paint certain things. One brush can be used to create flower petals, while another makes spectacular shrubs. The angle brush can create a perfect beard in quick time.

You should have a blank canvas available to just practice brush strokes. You will learn how to make each stroke so the effects are beautiful. Do not get discouraged if you do not get it right the first time. With practice comes familiarity. The more familiar you are with a brush, the better of a tool it becomes.

One technique which works well to help become familiar with how a brush handles is to try painting a picture only using one brush. You will quickly become familiar with what the brush can do and what it will not do. This is an old trick used by some teachers to help the student understand the limitations of each brush.

Chapter 4 – Creating Colors

What has always fascinated me about paints is the way you can blend them to create new colors. I have sat for hours with my palette and created many different colors all from three basic, primary colors. To me it was like opening a present to see what would happen if this color was blended with that color. By the time I was done, my palette had the makings of an English garden in full bloom, not to mention the exotic birds contained within.

There are stunning portraits and eye stopping canvases being created all the time with color. This does not have to be the case. The portrait can be just as stunning when done with the absence of color. Black and white always gets your attention.

You are the creator of the world on your canvas. You can have it as simple or complex as you wish. You can have it be formal or funny. If black and white what you like, then do black and white. If color is the key, then add all the color you wish. You will enjoy the piece more by allowing yourself to just let go and create.

Do not ever worry about whether something looks right or not. As one professional art teacher always stated, there are never any mistakes on the canvas, just happy accidents.

There is one thing you should remember when painting, keep the darks to the shadows. This means you can use the darker colors as a base for the lighter ones and the subject matter will actually shadow it's self. Of course, if you cover the entire dark area with the lighter color then adding the dark background is a mute point.

There are so many things which can be done with color. I once did an entire landscape using two colors, white and Prussian blue. It was a snow scene centered around a lake. I have to admit, it was beautiful. I am not the only one who thought so. I had it done exactly one hour and someone walked in and bought it right off the easel.

Nowhere in the world is the statement "Beauty is in the eye of the beholder" more true than in the art world. I have no desire to own a Picasso. To be honest, Norman Rockwell is more my style. In the world of art, there has to be something for everyone. That is what makes it such a grand adventure. Everyone has the ability to shine.

Colors allow you to turn a forest into a fall scene. Colors are what make certain portraits more noticeable than others. For instance, Thomas Kinkade has become one of the foremost artist's in this decade. He uses lighting and a warm color palette to create a canvas you would love to walk into. You can see more of Kincade's work at his web site, Thomas Kincade Gallery

Never underestimate what colors can do to an image. Always remember your lighting as well.

Chapter 5 – Where Is Your Light Source?

In the real world, the light comes from one main direction. This is the rule. Even if you are outdoors, the light from the sun comes at you from East to West. Depending on where you are during the day will determine where the shadows are. This is the same with painting.

You must always determine where your light source is coming from. Once you have done this, keep it consistent. It will show quickly if you have a subject standing on one side of the canvas with the light dancing off her hair from the left and on the other side of the canvas the table has light streaming in from the right.

You can help to keep the light source in the proper perspective by setting a light where ever you are going to have it shine from. If you choose to have the light source come from the right of the painting, then set a light to the right of your canvas. Keep the light source in your studio the same as the light source in your painting. This can assist you in keeping shadows where they need to be and reflective light where it should be.

As you become more familiar with painting you may not need this technique so much. It is just a simple way to keep everything flowing in the same direction. It helps to keep the visual real.

The light source will fade as it travels across the canvas. In some paintings, it will fade quickly. This will depend on the subject and type of painting you are doing. You may want to splash a sunset across the canvas. There will be shadows, and dark ones, where the light source starts to fade.

To understand how crucial lighting is in a painting, set up a still life on a table. Nothing fancy, just a few pieces of fruit in a bowl or a vase of flowers will do. Now get bare 60 watt light bulb to set around the table. Start on your left. See where the light glistens off the surface of the subject. Notice where the shadows are. See how the light fades across the scene.

Move the light to the back, front, and other side to notice all the angles. This will give you a good idea how light works on a subject. You can even simulate high noon by suspending the light bulb from up above. Placing a sheet or other translucent material between the light and the table will show you the affects of an overcast day or diffused lighting.

You can become familiar with lights and shadows the more you do this. By using different test models, you will begin to understand how curves, reflective surfaces, and other things can affect the light. This will enable you to capture it more accurately on your canvas.

If you thought all you needed to do was buy some paint, a brush, and a canvas to start painting you were right. To be really good at it takes some thought and planning. Even a few exercises in technique will be necessary to create a good work of art.

Chapter 6 – Your Painting Style

We are going to cover styles and techniques in this chapter. You need to understand the different forms of painting. You may find yourself drawn to one form or another. This often happens when you start painting. As you become more familiar with techniques, you will generate your own style.

There have been many different art periods. Here is a list of the periods along with some of the artists which made it famous.

1) Baroque – Caravaggio, Carracci

2) Classicism – Mengs, Ingres

3) Cubism – Picasso, Braque

4) Expressionism – Beckmann. Dix, Munch, Kandinsky

5) Fauvism - Matisse

6) Impressionism – Renoir, Monet, Pissarro, Morisot, Bazille

7) Realism – Caravaggio, Velazquez, Zurbaran

8) Renaissance - Michelangelo

9) Romanticism – Gericault, Delacroix

10) Surrealism – Arp, Ernst, Masson,Tanguy, Dali

Each one has its own unique style. Some are more of an impression than an actual picture, like a representation of what the artist feels about an issue or subject. At times this is referred to as abstract art. You can recognize the Romanticism type of artwork by the attention to detail. The background is left in shadow while the image is bold and clear. Human bodies are painted to represent each curve and muscle. The strength comes through without any doubt as to what the artist is trying to instill in the viewer's mind.

By choosing a style or form of artwork, you can have a reference to what your paintings will be representing. You can show the images you want.

Your likes and dislikes will show when you put them on a canvas. Whether you are a romantic or an impressionist, people who study your work will be able to tell at a glance.

You do not have to limit yourself to one style. There may be times you feel like painting just for the sheer joy of painting. When this happens, there is no telling what you will put on the canvas. As long as your feelings and desires come through in the artwork, it is just fine.

You may find it easier to express yourself when you put paint to canvas. There may be times you are depressed. You may find yourself in a state of joy and happiness. You will see these emotions come out in the artwork you are creating. This is what painting is all about. Creating a picture of what is going on in your mind, allowing others to see what you are feeling; these are the real reasons for painting. The fact that you enjoy watching a blank, white surface turn into something spectacular is a benefit as well.

No matter what style you choose, there is one which is right for you. You will decide this when you are more familiar with how you like to paint.

Chapter 7 – What To Paint About

For everything in this world there is someone who has painted it. Whether it is a person, place, or thing somewhere someone has put it to paint. It does not matter what you choose as your subject, as long as you feel comfortable painting it.

Some of the better subjects are ones that will offer color and contrast. For instance, a bowl full of bananas with an apple in the center. A vase full of blooming flowers is the perfect still life because of the colors and shapes.

You should look for many things when choosing a subject. If it is a landscape, you want some texture. What I mean is there should be different buildings, trees, or animals to add interest to the picture. You do not want to saturate the painting with activity but you do want to keep it interesting.

A scene which is full of busy people can be good as long as the activity stays in one place on the canvas. Making the background as busy as the foreground can over stimulate the senses. By adding the activity to a tranquil background, the painting takes on a sense of order.

You may choose to do portraits. Do not underestimate the subject. There is a term, "photogenic", which means that someone's beauty shows through the lens. You may see someone as plain and uninteresting. Under the eye of the camera, this person can transform into a vision of beauty.

The camera is the perfect tool to choose a subject. By taking pictures of what you want to paint, you can determine the contrast, lighting, and textures. You will be able to see what the view will look like framed. This can give you a better understanding of what you are really looking at. Taking a picture will show you the true view.

Another reason an artist may take a picture of their subject is timing. If you are doing a portrait, you may not be able to finish before the person has to leave. Even a boat in the harbor will put out to sea sometime, leaving you with an empty pier. The lighting changes every minute of every day. By taking a picture of the subject, you can preserve the moment so the painting can be done at your leisure. Even if you are using artificial lighting, there could be other circumstances which do not allow you to finish your work. The camera can become your new best friend when it comes to painting.

It can actually be fun taking pictures of different subject matter. Then you get to go home and choose which angle will make the best painting. You can experiment with lighting in this manner as well. By shooting from all angles, you can get many different views. There may be something the camera saw that you missed. Accidents can sometimes make the best artwork.

Never overlook anything when it comes to choosing a subject. One of the most intriguing art subjects I ever saw was a dandelion which had gone to seed. The artist had shot a close-up of the puffy seed head. He then painted it in shades of blue. It took several people almost three days to determine exactly what the subject was. Yet the painting fascinated all of us for quite some time.

Chapter 8 – A Place To Paint

There are certain things you will need for your studio. The first thing is a place to paint. Every beginning artist seems to think they can bring out everything and scatter it onto the kitchen table, set up an easel, and start painting. This is great for a day or two. If you want to continue pursuing an art career or hobby, you need a place to keep everything up and ready to go. This way, any time you feel inspired all you need to do is pick up a brush and start painting.

There are some basic things you will need for your studio or work area. The first of which is a table. Many times it is actually nice to have this be a desk with drawers. You can store extra supplies in the drawers for easy access.

You will also want an easel. There are some artists who are comfortable with painting on a flat surface. Most prefer the canvas at eye level. This means supporting it somehow. An easel is the easiest way to accomplish this. I have found that two or more easels are necessary. This makes it more accommodating to work on more than one piece at a time. You can choose from a table easel or a full standing easel. The table easel is good for someone who is limited in their ability to stand. It allows them to sit with the canvas at a comfortable level. Both types of easels are adjustable so the canvas can be raised or lowered accordingly.

Some artists have a set of shelves or shelving unit to store extra canvases, brushes, and other paint supplies. You can also keep completed paintings vertical and free from damage with an adjustable storage unit which allows the paintings to stand. One word of advice, never store turpentine, linseed oil, or other mediums of this type on the same shelves you store your completed work. Accidents have been known to happen. Should one of these bottles spill onto your work it could be ruined for good.

Beside your work easel, you will want to have a small table or cart. This will allow you to keep the items you need to complete the art work. You never know when you may need another dab of paint on your palette. You will also be able to set the palette down on a surface which will not be damaged if paint gets on it. Believe me when I say the paint does not only go on the canvas.

You will need a good supply of clean rags. Also necessary is a bucket or coffee can for clean up. You will most likely need many more than one, just to let you know. Jars work too, but can create a big mess when one falls and breaks. Metal cans are actually safer in the studio. Many an artist has gotten lost in their creation and backed right into a shelf or table, knocking everything down.

One of the most important things is a good lighting system. You will want to be able to see your painting in full light. This will allow you to see how the paint is going on the canvas. It will also make it possible to see the true colors you are using. The brighter lights should be set up by the easel. The more conventional lighting should be placed by the subject.

Once you have this all set up you are ready for the supplies.

Chapter 9 – Painting Supply Resources

There are many places you can find your painting supplies. Local craft stores and artist supply houses will have many of the supplies you are looking for. When you want it to come to you, there is always the Internet. You need to compare prices when shopping on line for your paint supplies. Here is a list of some of the better web sites that carry an excellent variety of artist's tools.

Blick Art Supplies

ASW Express

Mister Art

Jerry's Artarama

There are so many things you will want to get. It will be like a kid in a candy store to look at all the wonderful items for sale. It is best when you are first starting out to save some money and purchase student paints. This will allow you to become with the different mediums without breaking your wallet. You can build up your stock a little at a time. The paints actually go a long way. You just have to become familiar with your paints to understand thinning and liquefying. Very few times will you use paint straight out of the tube without mixing it with another color and some turpentine, linseed oil, or turpenoid.

The oils or additives also act as an aid in drying the oil paints. You do not need to worry about this if you are using acrylics. They are designed to dry quickly. An amusing note of interest is what your tubes of paint will go through when painting.

New paint tube   Old paint tube

You may think this will never happen to you. It happens to all of us all the time. You just have to get used to it. My mother was a professional artist for over thirty years. I still have visions of her coming out of her studio with paint up to her elbows, holding a squished up little tube and muttering about only needing an "itty bitty dab of the stuff". It was when this happened more than three times in a week that we went to the art shop to pick up more paint.

Chapter 10 – Cleaning Up

This is always the worst part in an artist's life. The need to clean up the palettes, brushes, easels, and other odds and ends in the studio. It is actually rather easy if you know what you are doing.

The brushes are the first thing to address. This is where the coffee cans come into play. Filling them half full of turpentine or other paint solvent will allow the brushes to soak until you are done with everything else. Just drop them in, bristle first, right into the turpentine. We will get back to these in a moment.

If you are working with oils, you will want a fine cloth to cover your canvas. Do not use a cloth which has a lot of lint or loose fibers. Thin cotton sheeting is perfect. Be careful not to let the fabric touch the art piece. You can actually buy extender clamps to attach to your canvas at the top. This allows the covering to drape without coming in contact with the painting.

The next thing you need to determine is if you are going to be using the same palette colors again, any time soon. If you are, then just slip the entire thing into a plastic bag and twist the end shut. This keeps foreign matter from getting into your paints while you are away.

If you have decided you are done with that particular color palette, scrape it off with a putty knife. I will say this about palettes. Stored properly, the ones you have used for your oil paintings will last for several days or even a week or so. You may not wish to waste the paints. If you are scraping the palette, rinse it off with some linseed oil or mineral spirits when you are done. Rub clean with a clean rag.

After you have put away all your supplies you can go back to the brushes. Certain brushes can carry a large paint load. You may not believe it until you are trying to clean them. Clean one brush at a time. Work the turpentine or other solvent into the bristles of the brush. Rinse with fresh solvent and completely dry with a clean rag. Either lay the brush flat or stand it up in a container with the bristles towards the ceiling. You do not ever want to leave the brush in solvent overnight. This can break down the brush and it will not perform as you have come to expect. Keeping the brushes clean and the bristles straight will allow them to continue making the brush strokes you want.

Acrylic paints can be cleaned up in the same way. However, the difference is the palette will not last. It must be cleaned after each use. The paints will dry within hours. There is one little tip that some artists use. By sticking the palette in a plastic bag and putting it in the freezer, the paints can stay soft. Sometimes this works and sometimes it does not. The quality of the paints has quite a bit to do with this.

Chapter 11 – Free Painting Lessons

The more you know the better you will become as an artist. For over 20 years, my mother taught many students the art of painting. She spent hours going over lighting, shading, and focal points. She taught about centering the eyes of the face instead of sticking them in the forehead. She explained color theory, paint mediums, and different brush strokes. She taught anyone who would listen. There were only two years she taught professionally. All the other times the lessons were free. She would say a gift is a gift. You do not charge someone to perfect a gift; you teach them to use it. It was perfect when God gave it to them.

There are other artists who feel the same way. Many different classes are offered on line and in the local community which are free. Here are some of the ones which are on the Internet.

Art Graphica

John Hagan Lessons

<u>Expert Village</u> This is probably one of the best because from a drop down menu, there are many on line videos with free access.

<u>Creative Spotlight</u>

You will find there are many others available. These should give you a great start to painting on canvas. There are lessons on using every medium. Each of them is from a different perspective because each is from a different artist.

The local library in your area and some other organizations usually has free art lessons at different times of the year. Check in the local paper to determine if there may be an organization offering free classes. You should never pass up the chance to learn about art.

As you learn, do the same for others. Never forget to pass on the lessons you have learned in your experience as an artist.

Chapter 12 – Caring For Your Artworks

An oil painting is not just some poster type thing you purchased at the local super store. It is an expression of someone's thoughts, feelings, or personal life. It is beauty and style with a sense of personal-ism. An oil painting is someone's creation. With proper care, your painting can last for generations.

You should never touch the painting it's self. Always handle it by the frame. Never allow anything to come into contact with the back or front of the painting, either. A canvas is pliable and can easily tear or have a hole poked into it.

In order to clean an oil painting, you should give it a light dusting with an extremely soft brush. Do not use sprays or chemicals on it at any time. Should there be damage or a dirt spot which is not able to be taken care of, have it repaired or cleaned professionally. You may think you are capable of doing this; however there are professionals who have been trained to handle original art pieces valued into the thousands. They know what they are doing.

Do not hang an oil painting in direct sunlight. This can fade the paint. It is advisable to hang the painting in an area with a rather constant temperature. Great changes in temperature can damage the painting over time. It is never advisable to hang an oil painting near an outside door or a window which is opened frequently.

For short storage or transporting, you can put cardboard on both sides of the canvas and wrap the entire painting, frame and all, in bubble wrap. A wooden crate with a moisture proof filling is recommended for long term storage or major shipping.

If you want to, when you have your painting framed, you can ask the framer to put the artwork under glass. This will ensure the risk of damage is at a minimum.

Chapter 13 – Attention to Detail

The picture above is an actual print done by my mother. This piece was taken from an oil painting she had done. You can actually see the canvas marks when you look closely at it. Look closely at this piece. The name of the painting is "Seaside Greeter". It was one of her last works she did before her passing. There are some things a new artist can learn from studying another artist's work. By studying this painting you can learn a great deal about contrast and lighting. You can begin to understand colors and shading. You should also get a sense of how to balance out a painting.

The first thing I want you to notice is the subject. The point is that *is* the first thing you notice. You know what she was painting. All the other things take a back seat to the blue herring. Although you notice the sand and the waves, this is not what is important. You can see the ocean behind the bird. Yet it is not impressive enough to distract from the subject. The sea shells on the beach do not compete at all with the subject. The only thing you see is the blue herring. Why? Because this is what the artist wants you to focus on. This is what the artist was entranced with when she painted this picture. She was fascinated with the proud stance these birds sometimes have.

She loved the subtle natural shading of their feathers. She also loved the way the eyes seemed to have a blank stare and still had a look of intelligence to them.

This painting was done in stages. The background of the ocean and sky was put in first. There was a great deal of color and blending that went on to get the right affect of the clouds and the water. More paint was added to the bottom of the canvas in other shades and hues. The paint was blended into the front of the picture to bring in the sand and beach. After the background had dried, the artist started painting the bird.

Being able to judge perspective and set a reference point is important for size composition. You have to look at what you are painting to understand where it should go in the picture. If you do not choose the size and placement carefully, it can cause a low quality painting. By paying close attention to detail you can create a masterpiece like the one above.

Some things to notice about this piece.

1) The horizon is blended perfectly and yet there is a definite distinction between the sky and the water.

2) The light source is directly above. Nothing is in shadow.

3) The artist was still careful to keep with the reality of the scene by making sure the waves reflected the color of the sky.

4) Not many things in nature are without a flaw. The artist was able to paint what she saw with the broken sea shells and ruffled feathers. This makes the piece even more realistic.

5) Using different brush techniques, she was able to capture the essence of the sand at the bird's feet. This did not take as long as some thought. When you know what a brush can do, you can make it perform.

I hope looking at this piece can teach you some basics in oil painting.

Chapter 14 – Your Subject Matters

There is one thing any artist must do when first learning to paint on canvas. This is to choose subjects which interest him. In other words when you are painting something you do not like, it will show.

The quality of the painting will not be as good as the others you have done. You will not pay as close attention to the details because you will want to hurry through and get it done. This will result in a poor quality painting.

Compare the two pieces of art work. My mother did them both. She loved the blue herring and hated owls. Can you tell? Anyone who is familiar with her work can take one look at this piece and know she did not enjoy doing it. There is more detail paid to the leaves than the baby owl.

When you like what you are painting, you will do very well. Stick with what you like to paint and leave everything else to the other artists. Do not compromise your quality for any reason.

Compare this piece to the owl. Now compare it to the first blue herring. The artist was able to capture the essence of the bird in this painting. She focused completely on the bird with no attention to the background at all. With subtle shading added to the background color, which is barely noticeable, she was able to show the light source coming from the left. By focusing on the bird, the viewer can sense a feeling of tiredness. To be honest, this bird is much older than the one in the first picture. The artist was able to capture this feeling. Yet there is still something proud in the way the bird is holding himself. One other note of interest. By putting the bird on a section of fencing, it gave the painting some level of grounding. There does not have to be a lot of detail in the background in order for the painting to be noticed.

Chapter 15 – Frequently Asked Questions

1) ___What is the best type of brush to use for painting?___ There are many kinds of brushes. Each one has a certain brush stroke. You will need to experiment with the different types of brushes. You can choose either sable hair, hog hair, camel hair, or synthetic.

2) ___Is a synthetic brush better than a natural hair brush?___ This is all a matter of preference. Some of the newer synthetic brushes last longer than the natural hair brush.

3) ___How can I choose a subject?___ It is best to choose a subject which inspires you. Finding something to paint is not the problem. Finding a subject you like will show in your work.

4) ___Should I do landscapes or portraits?___ Some artists are better at portraits than landscapes. They have the ability to capture the personality of the people they paint. Other artists can paint a landscape which looks as if you are looking out a window. Try one subject and then do another. Determine which you

enjoyed more. Also look at them both objectively and choose which one you feel it better. This will help in your decision.

5) ***What is a still life portrait?*** A still life, by definition is any inanimate object. This can be a flower, a bowl of fruit, or even a paper clip.

6) ***Why should I take pictures of my subjects?*** By taking a picture of your subject, you can have a better view of the subject. You can see it from varying angles. You will be able to use the photographs as a reference when painting. There are times when you may be painting a portrait and the model cannot stay for the entire session. If you have photographed the subject, then you can continue to work. Another property the camera can offer is the lighting effects. You can see where the light falls and where the shadows are. You will be amazed at what the camera can pick up that the naked eye does not notice. There are times when you may feel the subject is all wrong for the painting until you view it from a camera lens.

7) *Is there a special brand of paint I should use?*
Each brand of paint has its own unique
properties. You can experiment with each one
to determine which ones you prefer. There is
no one brand which will offer everything.
Some have more colors than others. Some are
more able to blend. Dry times can be different
as well. When you find one brand that works
for you, then you will know it.

8) *How can I store my unused paints?* Acrylics
do not store well after they have been put on
the palette. They tend to dry quickly. There is
one trick that can be done but the results vary.
You can cover the palette with plastic and
freeze it. There are times this will work and
times it will not. For the oils, you can cover
them with plastic as well. You can also
submerge them in water for later use.

9) *What are the benefits of acrylic paints?*
Acrylic paints have a quick drying time. This
means you can actually start, finish, and
possibly frame a painting all in one day. With
oils it can take days for the paint to dry.
Acrylics can blend and mix just as well as the
oil paints. Some artists prefer the acrylics to
the oils and vice versa. The acrylics can also be

built up. This can actually give you an almost three dimensional look on the canvas.

10) ***Does it matter how thick I put the paint on the canvas?*** You should never put more paint on a canvas than you need to. The paint has to dry between layers or you could have problems with flaking and cracking. The painting can be built up to generate the look you want.

11) ***Why did my painting crack?*** The more paint you have on a canvas means the more space the paint has to cover. As an artist layers paint on the rule of "fat over lean" applies. This means the paint has more medium mixed in with it as each layer is added. The addition of the oil makes the paint more flexible. This means there is less chance of the painting cracking as it dries.

12) ***Is there a way to seal my painting after it is done?*** When you have completed a painting you will want to seal it to make sure smoke, dust, and other foreign matter does not damage it. You can varnish the painting. You need to make sure the painting is completely cured before sealing. Also, the varnish should be a very thin coat of clear varnish. A thick

coat can cause the paint to appear yellowed as time goes by.

13) ***Why don't my paintings look natural?*** We see things in three dimensions. The painting should reflect this. In order to achieve this, as in a landscape, start with the background first. This means the entire background, from the sky to the grass. Then you would go in and add the mountains or distant tree line. You always need to work from the back to the front to give the painting more realism.

Chapter 16 – Art Schools & Programs

There are colleges everywhere that have an art program. Each one can offer great instruction. If you are planning to attend a school for their art program always determine what the curriculum is and what degree you can earn. Some only offer an associate's degree while others can offer much more. You will have to make the choice as to what you want from the school. Here is a list of art schools to consider.

The Art Institute of Pittsburgh

The Art Institute of Chicago

To find other art institute's you can go to the ART Institute web site. There are many all over the country and in Canada.

University of Texas: College of Fine Arts

Carnegie Mellon's College of Fine Arts

There are many other fine art schools available both with campus learning or on line classes. Each one offers financial aid to its students. The ability to further your education is possible. Speak with a campus advisor to determine your needs.

Chapter 17 – Museums of Fine Art

Throughout the world there are many places to see some of the greatest works of art ever produced. You could spend days in these fantastic exhibition halls studying the styles and techniques of some of the greatest artists who ever painted. Here are a few to get you started.

Museum of Fine Arts, Boston

Philadelphia Museum of Art

The Metropolitan Museum of Art

The Museum of Fine Arts Houston

Many of the fine arts museums offer partial showings of their exhibits on the Internet. You can appreciate the beauty of the paintings at home. This also allows you to view more museums which may not be as close to you.

Chapter 18 – The Joy Of Painting

There are many people all over the world who have aspired to become great artists. Many have succeeded. None have failed. For each person in their own unique way is an artist. Whether you create the picture with paint, pencil, or computer graphics the point is you are creating. You are expressing yourself in a way that is enjoyable to you.

Others may find great inspiration in your work. Criticism will always come, whether it is from others or even yourself. Do not let it bother you.

Art is a way of expressing our thoughts, feelings, and emotions. We can show who we really are by what we put on the blank canvas. This can sometimes be extremely thought provoking. It can be comical or whimsical. The point is that it expresses something. You capture the essence of who you are when you begin to paint.

Even if you cannot afford to make a living out of painting, do it for the joy of it. Do it because you find a love for painting. Do it every day. This is your time to shine. Let everyone know you painted that picture on your wall. Tell them you were the master artist when they ask where you got it. Let them know you can tell your story by the pictures you create.

Painting is a way of loving what you do *and* doing what you love. Remember, a picture is worth a thousand words, no matter how it is displayed.

Printed in Great Britain
by Amazon

73209315R00037